MW00676174

Siera,

Thank you so much
for your kind
listening.

Peace and blessings,

[signature]

02/18/16

THE
ILL
LAD
AND
THE
ODD
MC

Poems by Michael Moriarty

© Copyright 2009 by Michael Moriarty
All rights reserved.

First Edition

ISBN 0615277829

No part of this book may be reproduced or
transmitted in any form without prior permission
from the publisher.

Requests for permission or any other information
should be directed to the publisher.

Avabella Press
A division of Avabella Productions,
4299 Katie Jo Ct., Ann Arbor, MI 48103

Book design and cover photography by
Saroyan Humphrey

For Erik and Alden, my family, and Kristin

Contents

I.
THE
ILL
LAD

Kelly and The Van

What the hell, Mom?

You don't just walk over
with a big dumb helpful smile on your face
and ask Kelly, my heart stammering 5th grade crush,
a blonde halo swing set angel,
if she would like a ride home with us.

This is maybe something we could have discussed!?

My panic frozen face
reflects off the smudge coated window
of our 1994 Ford Aerostar.
A rust eaten eyesore of mini-van oblivion
with flies feasting on the shame inside.
A testament
to the failure of American engineering
She's coming this way.
This is not happening.

In better days
I dreamt when I got up the courage
I'd walk her home
and we'd both blush as I told her
I'd been desperate to say how pretty she is
since she tagged me that one time during recess
and she'd say *you're sweet*
and we'd hold hands
and maybe
on the last day of summer
we'd kiss in her driveway
and I'd be a man at just 11 years old
and my life would be complete
so far ahead of schedule

but instead,

she's going to see how we live.
She, the privileged daughter of restaurant owner,
brand name clothes, no hand-me-downer.
She's just hopped on into our gallery of white-trashery
where decay reigns supreme.

Where fast food grease bags crumple in every corner.
Sesame seeds swarm like insects – everywhere.
Where we feature mystery stains on the ceiling
like coffee, yet somehow, still sticky?
A playing card jammed in an air vent.
Gym clothes mountain pouring over seat-backs.
Coke cans drooling onto her feet. She
soaks in our garbage.

I can't see her expression
and I'm too terrified to speak, as Mom
makes small talk. *How's your family?*
I'm panicking, I'm
praying we'll crash,
as she finds out how my family is
a testament to the failure of American engineering.

There will be no walking her home
with confused hands and jittery eyelashes.
I begin to hope she'll pity me.
The poor boy from down the street
who couldn't pull himself up by his bootstraps
(his bootstraps being lost somewhere
in the back of this van).

After a sweaty eternity,
she said a luminous goodbye
and I whimpered mine.
Riding home in the dirt of silence,
I retreated into the clean, safe, lonely,
vacuum of my head.
Where I would spend the rest
of this long, long
childhood.

The night we met you asked me to write a poem for you.

Your eyes were glowing exit signs when you told me
your childhood was your father's fist through whitewall was
watching your mother paste colostomy bags
to her cancer cut husk was unjust.
Your childhood was a promise
that god didn't keep.

Now you deserve a poem like
summer nights deserve cricket symphonies.
You deserve the sky to crack
and rain down apologies like butterflies.

Your razor scars looked like lines in my journal
and I never wanted to write again
until these words were welded over your wrists.
You are a lit match tumbling toward the gasoline
pooled in my stomach.
When you slash your skin
I'm stabbed split helpless.
I can't let this be.

You don't think you're beautiful
(a plague of flute notes spooled through my throat).

These knives like thoughts surge through your crown,
and one day you will stop taking them by the blade.
A blue stone strength swells at your center
and you will know beautiful --
the strange engines of seeing churn in you.

And I can pour song from the thick nimbus I've been lost in
since your breath coalesced into my skull
and I will tell you the exact co-ordinates
on your back where I lost my mind

but you will learn to love the soft coastline
where your freckles island
without me, without anyone else.

Still, my eardrum's rapture -- your laughter
when you call me Books Moriarty,
or when I tickle just above your kneecaps
until, salt, silt, and breeze
lace your cheeks -- quenching something deep.

This poem is you softening moments from sleep
sinking beneath an ocean of scars
and into open arms.
There is no mirror with mouth enough
for the burst stretched sigh of the tired bell
of your body
and if my tongue is more than ballast in my skull
it was meant to trace the valley
where your hips dive to meet your waist
to translate the space, the curve, the yearning,
the taste of god, the pain that carved,
the love handles, and the love that they hold.
You dance and you laugh
when I try to
so dance like this is your poem,
like the hymns in your veins have caught fire
and cherubs are ripping out your hair. Dance
like a velvet goldmine exploding. Know, your breath,
a white rose risen through rubble of gums and ash of tongue
that throws petals in the wind to drift slow.
This is my small offering,
a conjugation of your lip print blooming from my cheekbone.
This is your poem
and your eyes are two harvest moons in the arms of a forest.
Just so you know
there is timorous water that longs to hug your ankle bones,
and one day you will dance through puddles of heaven
that echo
welcome home.

Wading

Every time we visit
Grandma thinks I'm someone else.
Today, I'm her brother.
She reminds me
of the time we hopped the downtown trolley
that clattered off old Detroit stone
then watched the sky blush on our picnic blanket
and spent the breath of evening on the riverfront
wading into twilight.

Dad frowns motionless in the corner.
Head cradled in hands searching
for a memory he can squeeze
around Grandma like a life preserver
because she cannot tread water
any longer.

I wish he didn't look so scared.
I'm not used to demolitions this close — his silence
echoes of brick crumbling
red dust in the wind
and metal snapping like toothpicks.

I look down to the symmetrical oblivion of the hospital tile floor.

In the muted car ride home
I can't peel this tension from my skin.
Chris asks mom why dad is crying
and I wish he would just shut up because
I don't want to know or hear that choking sound
like he can't breathe.
The air — turning liquid.

Dad spends a lot of time alone.
I think he's planning how to ease grandma
into the cool bubbling twilight

but the current is too strong,
and they're losing their grip.
Some days, I'm afraid they'll both be swept away
and I'll be left on the banks
to neatly fold up memories
and carry them home.

Learning to Watch My Step
After Phillip Levine

For Ed

To keep your joints from freezing
you walked our neighborhood constantly.
You took shelter beneath the staircase to West Park
and when I walked it I could see
a plume of rotten purple sleeping bag
and a plastic Wonderbread wrapper
spilling out from your hovel of aching wood.

Sometimes when Mom and me pulled weeds
in the front yard, you'd pass and say
Mary, keep that boy busy
and when I was 10 you stopped me.

We sat on opposite park benches.
You coughed ash flecks into your beard
and I was nervous — kicking cigarette butts
and looking at my feet. Your face
was chewed by shrapnel, and your bruised voice
staggered me. You said, *West Park is beautiful at dawn*
and I could hear you breathe like the city
was resting on your chest.
You told me about dropping out
of everything and drinking your way into
a deep place you couldn't leave.
I can't say we were friends,
but I respected you and wasn't sure why or to what end.

I watched you circle the block, shivering,
from behind our dining room window
fogged with heat – you showed me a truth
that I hope will never soak into me.

I walked on top of where you'd sleep
and wondered if you were there
beneath, those moments crushed in my stomach,
the sun hovering lonely.

You knew the shelter schedules
and which ones would still let you in. You knew
the band shell's depth, the places where the rain couldn't reach
and the many where it crept in.
You knew winter winds whipping brittle limbs
and that I would listen
and you could tell how much money in a man's pockets
by the man's walk but I never saw you ask for it —
your hands buried in dirty flannel.
I think you knew when I would die,
if I would be scared then
and if my face would show it
or if I would be warm and surrounded by good omens.

Once Mom invited you in,
we sat in the kitchen, over minestrone steam
I saw your shoulders slacken.
You reminisced on how
you dove in the Huron River from the bridge.
Mom handed you a wool hat and gloves
and wished you a merry Christmas.
Then you disappeared into distance
limping into a blizzard.

I will not forget you, practically next to my bedroom.
The night the ambulance carted you away —
frost bit, left foot, amputated
in the sick futility of sedation.
The last I knew of you was a bad winter and a siren.
Should I look down when I walk
over those steps where you once slept?
Should I picture you then, and where, and when?
I wonder where you've been, if your joints
are locking slowly like storm clouds, on a bench

next to your crutches, and a bottle, never to walk again.
I think you tried to hand me the sun rushing out over
the jagged teeth of buildings.
You were a pillar of crumbs, of small humanity,
a mouthful of raw nerve soaking,
a bladed gaze flashed at police like
what more can you take from me?

When the frost seeps in,
I wear too many layers to never release this heat.
I watch the sun laid to rest over West Park.
I go many places staring at my feet,
waiting for the concrete to whisper your footsteps to me,
unsure of what I see
in all the places you left empty.

Recoil

Darren was sweaty,
fat. His hair, matted
gold, shed dandruff on thick shoulders.
Gaze fixed on some fantasy novel
he would hurl himself into
like a stone.

There was no escape in this.
Dave, or Chris, or Jeffrey often
drew shame blushing to his bulbous cheeks.
In gym class they'd laugh, say,
Jesus, look at his fat legs...
        that's fuckin' disgusting.
                Hey Darren, why don't you run some laps?
                    He probably couldn't even finish one.

They'd teach Darren
an important lesson
about humans. How badly
we can injure.
Rather than beat him into submission
their dominance
was as simple
as popping
a balloon
with a needle.

He learned his place:
ugly fag, little bitch, fat homo,
who'd never touch
a girl who'd never
ball his sausage fingers
into a fist he just
learned to go limp and bury
tears beneath all those
layers.

For him to say, *you guys are jerks*
just meant more torment.
He learned to take it.

Sometimes I wished they would just hit him.
Make it real. Give him a bruise
he could wear so his parents wouldn't wonder
why he acted so weird,
why he flinched before he spoke
and never made eye contact with anyone.

I wish I'd been brave enough to stand up for him
but I was just happy he was fatter, weirder, and quieter,
than me.

When he was around
I was safe.

Every day he'd recoil
deeper into his head
like a dog that'd been hit by a car,
limping into an alley.

Every day I watched
silently.

Glad
it wasn't me.

I was a coward. He was a target.
A punching bag
for boys to practice becoming men
by bruising.

The day they broke him,
the same words this time snapped
him open, he was gulping huge breaths
like a goldfish
on a desk.

He choked,
just leave me alone
just leave me alone
slammed his fist
on the table
and tore out
of the room.

Jeffrey said, *what a baby.*
And I've never hated a person more
than how I hated myself
for watching this
and doing nothing.

A few months later
there was Columbine.
Two outcasts, fucked with
a few too many times,
started shot-gunning
their bullies away.

I remember
the torment tapered off that week,
Darren read his fantasy books in peace,
and I relaxed a little too.
Only fear could bring that much silence.

Weeks later,
Jeffrey was passing around an English assignment,
and Darren brushed his hand. He said,
don't touch me, queer.
And I knew everything would be back to normal.

Jeffrey said, *what...*
you aren't going to pull a Columbine, are you?
And I waited
knowing Darren
would not respond.

The Roller Rink

You show off your skating skills to the girls
because they are all you have. No style,
no charisma. All you can do to impress them
is deftly switch between sailing forward and backward.
Your sweaty batman shirt flails in the wind
and you swim through colored lights like smoke over kool-aid

but the girls are not interested. Your athleticism
does not compensate for a curled up bowl cut, baby fat clung
to cheeks like freckled tofu and skin too fragile to chance rejection.
You cut smooth crossovers at the corners, lean
into turns. A useless display. A ritual for disinterested goddesses.

You bump into some older kids. The boys spit
watch where you're going stupid and you don't stand up to them.

But still you will miss
the sputtering of your useless tongue like a deflating balloon.
You will miss the wind across your acne and bobbing your head
to songs you didn't know. You will miss the brittle dry cookies
you stomached after another solo flight.
You will wish they hadn't closed this place
before you ever got to roll across that golden sheet of time
while holding hands with a girl
who didn't care how fast you skated.

The Strawberry Fiasco in 2 Parts:
A Tragedy and a Battle Rap

I slunk into Slauson Middle School
in my hand-me-down disaster of
red tattered and stained sweat pants
with a red sweat shirt to match.

It was my understanding
that matching clothes were cool
and this was my first attempt.

My more fashionable peers
swiftly shelled out fifties
for their proudly sported Abercrombie & Fitch and American Eagle,
and looked down on my dingy outfit
like I was
a peasant

and that
sucked.

But this day
would harvest and devastate
my fragile pre-teen psyche

I sat in class
–quiet as usual–
to avoid drawing attention when...

Marcus Crowley —
vile demon child with ginsu tongue
that cut swift through self-esteem,
sent from the depths to smite me
a screeching phoenix of meanness
rising from the ashes of my happiness.
This boy had the audacity to present my plight to the class

as if it were central to the lesson plan.
HEY EVERYBODY, MIKE LOOKS LIKE A BIG FAT STRAWBERRY!

Uproarious laughter erupted.
Desks shook from the sheer amplitude of their cackles.
And as my embarrassment grew
like a ripe strawberry in bloom,
I blushed, the blood rushed to my face,
and this would prove to be my doom.
LOOK, HE'S BLUSHING, HE REALLY IS A STRAWBERRY!
My face - red, clothes - red
face - red, clothes - red.
Pores become seeds as sweat beads on my head.
Hair becomes green and sprouts leaves from my flesh.
Why hasn't the damn teacher started class yet?!
Somebody stop this nightmare.
Hide me in a shortcake, just get me the hell
out of here.

Of course those sweats now rest in
the dust of a forgotten dresser.
Never to be mocked again.
But as I sit here writing this
after years of shuddering at the thought of a matching sweat suit,
I stop to think,
why be so scared of being compared to a fruit? I mean...
we strawberries carry a history, sweeter than ordinary.

Check the recipe.
Bitch MC:

I'm valuable source of vitamin C, fiber, and potassium,
don't test me son.
I've long the felt scorn of privileged kids,
In fact, Strawberry Fields was an orphanage.
Mysterious? Argentineans once thought me poisonous.
I'm crazy as Darryl strawberry
sniffin' coke off a Strawberry Alarm Clock face.
I'm the bonus points in your Pac Man game.

Madame Tallien of the French Revolution
bathed in strawberries for radiant skin.
And the Norwegian municipalities
of Norddal and Kvaefjord rock
strawberries as their coat of arms and that my friends
is why everyone knows
not to fuck with Norwegians.

The fragrantly sweet juices and deep red hues brighten up the taste
and aesthetics of any meal.
I keeps it real.

Hey everybody! I'm a big fat strawberry!
and I'm just as sweet inside.
My every shape, sculpted as nature designed this
beautiful, fruitful existence.
I'll wear proudly the bruises of losers before me.
Don't step to me in bad taste.
And Crowley, you'll know I'm in season
when I serve you up homemade
some humble pie with rhubarb
then smash you with the plate.

II.
THE
RISE
OF
VERBAL
ASSAULT

Chesty

Hardcore
backdoor
on the floor
sex with Chesty
cause she's so zesty
and I wanna molesty...

This was the chorus to the first rap we ever wrote —
a love poem encoded in frustration and testosterone.

She sat at the table across from us at lunch time,
we drowned in her hair like molasses,
her curves unraveled our insides,
and her breasts were visions of paradise
for some more attractive guy.
Too terrified to look in her amber eyes
or give conversation a try we gawked in awe and silence —
certain that her body
was a treasure that losers like us could never caress...y.

But one day an epiphany just kicked in the doors to our minds:
We could profess our longing in rhymes,
we could imagine what it was like,
we could spit a better life.
I spent more time working on my 8 bars for this song
than I did on a week's worth of homework and on Friday night
we pulled our verses crumpled from overflowing backpacks.
After a few hours of bustin' moves
on the beta version of Dance Dance Revolution,
and after my parents went to bed,
I brought forth my Yamaha keyboard,
a blank tape, and my Mr. Microphone from when I was 6:
Then I tapped out a drum beat manually on the keys
kick kick snare, kick kick kick snare, repeat endlessly.
Three desperately horny 15 year olds
donning MC fantasies to be like Snoop and Master P

with gangsta lean
and hands on the asses
of their dreams.

We chanted rights of passage
a penthouse forum set to a beat —
all her parts to be licked and squeezed
backseats and whipped cream
give it to me and bitch please

bitch pleeeeeaasssseee...
(love me)

If she heard her song
I'm not sure if she would have given us the backhand,
turned and walked away, or sat stunned and disgusted.
But I do know this...
when Erik rhymed Chesty with *I'm from the mid-westy*
this night clamped forever onto my memory.

Our group name was the Animal Krackaz (with a Z!)
Alden was Skittlez, (with a Z!),
Erik was Reeze'z Piecez (with 3 Z's!!!),
and me, well...being that my initials were MM,
M&M's seemed appropriate to stick with the food theme,
but it turned out some guy was already using that name
so we settled on Verbal Assault.

Skittlez, Reeze'z Piecez, and Verbal Assault?!

Spitting game as only sweat stained, acne laced,
middle class rejects can —
stretching imaginations over the cracks in our tough guy masonry
and there could be no greater stretch
than that which would create and narrate
a 3 way between this lunchroom goddess, her equally beautiful friend,
and a boy who listens to Ludacris
while playing Magic: The Gathering.

O to be young and in lust.
To have friends with the same thin skin and big lungs.
To pretend thug. To say carpe diem.
Carpe deez nutz.
To know that you would grovel at her feet
if she just smiled at you but to demean her
because you're scared and dumb.
To be awkward and cuss.
So honest. So in a rush to grow up.
To swim from the capsized boats of our tongues,
vocalize the drums in our guts
and offer virgin prayers to one day fuck
dirty. To try and leave the shells of our boy
bodies
flaccid on the ground
like used condoms.

Special Moves

In the armor of youth,
guzzling night,
we shuffled through construction sites
in subdivisions we could never afford to live in.
We climbed the spiral staircase with no rail,
sword fought with two-by-fours
and whipped scrap metal
against the naked wood insides
till it stuck

or *fuck you's* trembled on our gas-station-slurpy-blue lips
beneath the Mobil's buzzing fluorescents.
We copped dollar cologne at the counter
it was our essence.
Fists for anyone against us...

We'd dare each other to ask out the Westside bartender
even though we were too scared
she would shoot our big talk down
to open mouths
and Happiness was an empty arcade,
was joy sticks and 2 buttons,
freakin' the X-men
eh eh eh eh X-men X-men
TORNADO CLAW!!!
(busting your special move lowers your health
save it for when you really need it).

Before pockets full of pharmaceuticals,
before robo-trips and nitrous,
before life sipped our insides through straws,
there was 4 teenage boys
fondling freedom in the back of Erik's Celica
and peeing on the side of his neighbor's house
because he wouldn't let us park in front.

Blurring night's and morning's borders,
we stomped through Meijer's sliding doors for combos
and caffeine.
In the parking lot —
battle carts and handfuls of sparks.
We squirted that nasty liquid candy crap
beneath the door handles of all the nicest cars —
our goo on their privileged fingers
like we existed
like we could touch them.

Trying to jam one of the carts into an abandoned car
was like fighting the impossible physics of future and distance

But the outcast stars found mercy for us,
and spray-paint cans lined the backseat carpet
like an arsenal of God's gifts to a squadron of misfits
who wrote *shit*, and *ass*, and *fuck*
on the rusted red doors and trunk
in celebration of
our small spectacle of nothing much.

I decided I could call myself a graf writer
cause it would be true
if *ass* was my tag.

We started home with Cheshire grins of pride flashed wide,
then Alden turned for one last look at our work,
took his dollar cologne from his pocket,

then launched it

square into a rear window
that completely shattered
into a perfect madness
and happiness was hey what the hell are you kids doing?
the dash into the dark,
and the adrenaline stuttered heart,
the unbelievable luck

to make it safely to the sidewalk
2 seconds before Erik's mom pulled up looking for us.

Breath blared in our chests like police sirens,
the dents we made — our sacred mayhem.
The debris of our safe sterile days at our feet,
we didn't wait for special moves,
we made them.

Would you like to try our new balls in the face program for just 25 cents?

I walk into Hollywood Video
and my boss says,
Michael, would you meet me in my office?
*We need to do some **role playing**...*

So we're in his office
and he says,
Let's hear your sales pitch for the new Playguard Program

and I wish he had just made a pass at me
like I'd thought initially
so I could have a more legitimate reason
to be this angry

because lots of people have to suggestive sell at their jobs,
it could be worse,
but it's not so much the push to purchase
that curdles the bile in my gullet,
it's having to constantly explain
what I'm selling.

Hello sir or madam,
would you like to try our new Playguard Program for just 25 cents?
I'll intone...

What is that exactly, young man?
They may ask.

Well, I'll tell ya! But you might wanna sit down. The Playguard Program
is the brainchild of some corporate think tank with a bunch of overpaid
shitgrinning idiots trying to figure out why 3rd quarter profits are down.
And rather than accept the natural fluctuations in people's spending habits
and the business drain of Net-Flix, they slapped together this wacky scheme
wherein I'm supposed to sell you, the guest (not customer, but guest), I'm

expected to sell you **DVD Insurance.**

Oh yeah...you heard me right, **DVD Insurance.**

Well, actually we like to call it a "Damage Waiver" because we don't want you to think you're committing to anything serious like insurance. Well, actually we like to call it "Damage Protection" because we don't want you to think that we hold you liable for the damage to our products. Well, actually we like to call it "Magic happy time fairy dust" because we trust our "guests" with our movies but nothing as serious as honesty. "DVD Insurance!?" You'd have to be some kinda slack-jawed rube to fall for that, but "Damage Protection," well, that's just downright frugal.

So here's the deal, John Q. Public, on the 1 in 100,000 chance that you happen to step on your precious rental copy of Wedding Crashers, cracking it beyond repair, your 25 cent investment will save you from the 15 dollar replacement fee. But wait, there's more! You'll also receive, free of charge, balls in the face! The invisible tea bag of the market, raked across your brow.

Not convinced? Well, how about this. Pretend you're riding the bus and I offer you "damage protection" for 25 cents, and the deal is—if you get mugged, your next ride is free.

Or try our Playguard program — imagine that you're throwing a quarter down a wishing well but it only comes true if your wish was to have one less quarter.

Not interested? Don't worry. I've got other exciting opportunities. Squander 75 cents of your hard earned pay and you'll be eligible for eyeball insurance. If they happen to pop out of their sockets while you're watching, you'll receive a free promotional cane from Grumpier Old Men.

Or wrist insurance. Let's say you pay 3 dollars and if you get Carpal Tunnels from rewinding to that part of Taking Lives where Angelina Jolie is totally naked, we'll send you that hand prop from the Addam's Family Movies.

Or if you really want value, and I'm talking top dollar, then why not go for the DVD insurance insurance? For just 5 dollars, we'll pay your medical bills after the inevitable rage induced brain aneurysm that will befall you when I explain what DVD insurance is.

But anyway, we're there in his office and I role play with the imaginary customer, betraying the urge to stab myself in the trachea with a ballpoint pen just so I never have to say these words again, but a few months after I quit, I get a letter, and it says therein:
To whom it may concern,
Hollywood Video Corporation has filed for bankruptcy
and everyone who's worked a shit job should get a chance to feel like this. To dance the dance of freedom atop the grave that greed dug itself with a golden shovel. Everyone who's ever been forced to ask if you'd like to try our new Fiesta Suprema Taco Salad or stood on the corner in a giant pizza slice costume should get a chance
to stand ankle deep in the ashes of the king's throne.
To calmly dial the phone, wait on hold to speak to the highest ranking official available and say
Hey, Hollywood Video,
would you like to try my new bankruptcy program?
It's where you go bankrupt
and this deal
is worth every   single   penny

Fahrenheit 400 Degreez: The Temperature at which Teenage Boys Burn

I picked my acne
then picked the scabs.
Peeled dry skin from my lips till blood ran.
My ears were way too big
and my front teeth overlapped.
But mostly, I was hormones.
Chaos and mad
erections in class.
So many pretty girls I could never
have – or talk with. Jaw wired by shyness.
13 with my feet wet in a pool
of MTV and desperate for acceptance,
from the TRL altar I ingested
Beauty. Charisma. Beauty. Charisma.
And dreamed of being like that.

When from the static mist arose
a mouthful of gold fronts
and an anthem:

Girl you looks good,
won't you back that ass up?
grabbed my testosterone soaked attention and lust.

You's a fine muthafucka
won't you back that ass up?
Raps cut through my quiet shell like *what.*
Juvenile rained from a cloud of weed smoke
the kind of swagger I needed yo.
In his video...asses wobbled in slow motion
synchronized with each jiggle
the dawning swelled like a sub woofer rumbling:

Juvenile is ugly

like
almost as ugly as me.
Glory.

The ice on his wrist glinted like confidence.
I copped that 400 Degreez and locked it in.
My nine was gonna ride with me
in flossin' season on Miller Street.
As if I could wrestle dirty south heritage around my ribs
and call it identity.
As if Uzi sputtering drums and fresh synths
could blow rhythm into this whiteboy chrysalis.
I was going through the motions of manhood
on some gangsta shit.

I threw my sets up. I mean...
I threw the west up cause it was the only one I knew how to do
but you better not speak on my K-mart clothes
cause I bust gats. I mean... I listen to tough raps.

I rocked soulja rags in history class.
I was gonna peel wigs back and sling some crack.
I was gonna pimp and smack.
I was gonna live at last. I was gonna sing and dance.
I was gonna piss my pants,
spit the facts, rip hot tracks
bridge this gap, and dip in black.
I was gonna bling and jack.
I was gonna click, click, blast.
I was gonna grip some cash.
I was gonna strip off this sadness, split this mask,
smoke spliffs of grass, sip Cris and Jac.
I was gonna get some ass.
I was gonna get some ASS!
I was gonna be like that.

I was gonna lip synch
everything I was missing.

I, Whiteboy

After Ben Alfaro

> "This was Hip Hop's whitest generation yet [...] and yet they
> never seemed to wonder what their proper place was — if they
> were lounging at tables marked reserved."
>   – ADAM MANSBACH, *Angry Black White Boy*

1.
Hip Hop doesn't need me.

2.
At rap shows I wonder
if I look stupid when I throw my hands in the air.
Like, *do I look weird? Gangly? Is the DJ back there laughing at me?*
Or do all white people
look inherently weird with their hands in the air?
Maybe we store racial tension and guilt in our shoulders.

3.
I cry listening to Death Cab for Cutie
frequently.
I played hockey –
Hockey.

4.
I can't freestyle. I can't break.
I can't graf-write. I can't DJ. I can
find justice in a courtroom, like an old relative
in a family photo. I can
relax when police pull me over. I can get a
just don't let it happen again for a marijuana offense.

This free ride is my inheritance.
This stolen land, these safe suburbs,
this head start, these ruptures along colors,

these are my inheritance.
It doesn't change if my ancestors
were not the ones
paving this way with rifles and chains
cause I still caught the windfall of privilege,
and I'm still playing a rigged game.

5.
I packed rap in the blender of my mouth,
shredded confetti
for the day I was no longer scared
to be me
and I am sorry
and honesty does not absolve me.

6.
I was reading Murderdog magazine.
Checking out the letters the readers sent in
responding to the coverage of Project Pat's recent stay in prison
and this guy was like,
We don't care about how he was eatin' right, or lifting weights,
what we wanna know is, how many whiteboys did he punch in the face?

I wore a Fubu sweatshirt
with the words *Dirty South* emblazoned on it
2 or 3 times.
This is probably the sort of thing
that would make Project Pat punch a whiteboy in the face.
Actually, it could provoke that response from a lot of people.
I'm pretty lucky I didn't get my ass knocked out.

6.66.
Side note: The whiteman is still the devil.
                    If you need an explanation,
                    you'll never understand it.

7. Fellow whiteys:
Let's shut up and learn some things.

Dig in the crates for some lessons:
Kool Herc, Bambaataa and Starksi.
But it won't make you special or anything.
If you get checked for being ignorant, take it as a learning experience.
I try to step to Hip Hop like an ugly dude stepping to a really fly girl.
In this analogy my ugliness is accentuated
by the 200 plus years worth of blood on my newly sagging jeans.

Don't talk to her unless she acknowledges you.
Just be happy if she lets you sit at the same lunch table.

If you get invited into the cipher, be grateful
cause you can be left out
like many peoples
out of history.

III.
SHRAPNEL

Pioneer High School: 2000

A girl folds into the great wide chest of a boy
I now hate because I have no good skin
for a girl to be folded in. I'm a pocket of air,
self-sustained by the tension of anger between
the hands, the heart, and the head.
A lucent stew of husks of kisses.
The students go by me.
They clatter and close circles.
A collage of distraction — bangles on a girl's wrist,
lipstick, headphones mumble distant.
A wash of tired faces. A thrum.

They clutch for bodies, something
like learning. A burst of perfume inflames me.
A boy boxes his friend's chest.
I float like dead flies in syrup.
An ambulant echo of *fuck you* and *I love you*
so only the *you* can be heard.

I live in a garret above two insomniac eyelids
who whisper *you're useless*,
back and forth every night.
In these halls I live a constant in-breath,
to grab a stranger, tell her my name
and ask her to be my friend.

A fat sad looking hall monitor scans everything.
I wonder if he sees me watching him. Before his walkie-talkie
crackles and sends him on what feels like purpose there will be static.
My lungs are full of static. The bell rings and is ugly so people
are going. The traffic pushes faster.

My body is less a cage than a novelty. Scabs to peel and
what seems like pleasure when I touch it right.
I can't remember the last time somebody touched me
and it makes me sad. Not even a stranger.

Not even two hands reaching for a door at the same time.
That random clasp. A reminder to the living.
My heart is a forgotten bomb threat.

A sudden knowing: if I stepped out of my body
I would not break into blossom, I would not be free,
because I am as far from my body as I can possibly be
like waving to myself in a mirror. And sometimes
I stare at myself in the mirror for what seems like a long time,
pressing the reflection to see if something will pour out.

In the hall today, laughter,
a wall of fucking laughter
in a crowd
I can disappear
like a silence
no one asked for.

So I ask the red tiles I stare at,
the desks I almost sleep on,
and this mass of people who will never know my name,
sweep the last tethers of tendon and brain to fray
and snap me wide away. Release me into this place
and out. Paint me a ghost jangling and sinking through.
A backdrift. A saint for a boy crying in the bathroom.
Will he feel my hand on his shoulder?
A crackle of static. A swirl along the fluorescent
lights that just decay down on everything. Release me
so I can be a janitor with a push mop for all my dirty thoughts,
and ache my way into this building.
So I can feel a hornets' nest riot in my stomach
an awful humming, too much to breathe.
So I can feel what it's like to be touched
in a thousand places at once. Even if it's not on purpose.
Even if everyone is waiting to leave.

We Left School
After Gwendolyn Brooks

and our backs thudded against brick — sank deep,
released. Where numbers, grades, and the teeth
of others couldn't reach. We donned headphones,
etched stars from cheeks, alone.
Just outside the view of teachers' windows.
A dull stone of silence in our throats, maybe
smoke, or just watching this gone world,
these buildings overgrown.
The saddest miracle we could ever hold.
Knowing we could sink away from this place like a shard of rust
from the edge of a tugboat and no one would ever know.
We close off like classroom doors,
learn something new every day.
A pair of shoulders shrinking. We try
to escape.

A Plea to Speak Before Shooting, to the Trenchcoat Mafia, the Question Mark Kid, and All Those Collapsing in the Back of our Classrooms.

Did you want to inject as much misery into our lives as you can, just because you can? – Cho Seung Hui

Show us we are wrong.
Show us you deserve this breath.
Show us the buckshot dove gone spiral into your chest.
Call out from the places where your head is caving in.
Unveil scraped nerves and barb
punctures from our teeth. We carved you ugly,
punched you *fucking loser*,
threw rocks at you walking home,
drove fists into your stomach,
watched you crumple.
We deserve to tremble
staring down the barrel and bullet, yes,
we pushed you to this
but you can do more.

Put the gun down, and save the others like you.
Let's face it, we never listened,
have no business asking forgiveness,
but how many outcasts nurse your same bruises,
how many pulling taut the same nooses
in bedrooms, the first pipe bombs bursting
in their skulls. Speak for those
who become bone shrapnel.
Splatter our brains with your story.
How many taught to hate their own bodies,
acne, sweat, and ragged clothes –
their faces pressed
on the glass we socialize behind

with cleaver mouths in flattering light.

Affix our careless stares to your gaze
to deepest nowhere.
Wear scars like funhouse mirrors
we see our ugly selves in.

A small good thing
to leave this world less blood soaked
than in your beginning.

Berate our privilege, silver platter slobber,
and arrogance, but you
can be an arm in the machinery of bullies grinding meat
to stop everything.

Speak that you know a TV better than your family,
and bury yourself in music, your stomach — a fuse lit —
you don't know what to do with it.
Tell us you sat silent
until the teacher forced you to read
in front of the class
and everyone laughed at your accent and numb
expression, chanting
go back to china.
We branded you fag, freak, psycho,
speak the strangled ego.
Teach us something —
the slouch of shy kid imploding,
your knuckles ground raw on the doors of friendship and acceptance,
the beauty and futility of desperate attempts for connection in
misguided sexual text messages
but do not waste your hardship
for one moment of savage catharsis.
Someone has to learn from this.

If we won't listen, there are others broken
waiting for a voice to crescendo over the smack of laughter
on the cheek of the fat kid over the smack of hammer to bullet.

Do not do this
and let us forget you
as another killer
we did some fucked up shit to
but we need no remorse for you
'cause you're not one of us anymore.
Don't let us say you were just insane
or that we were glad to see you leave.
Don't let us regret you,
as if a monster
is all you could have been
and all you will ever be.

Words He Didn't Want

This guy came into the Writing Center today
told me he was home from Iraq,
and handed me his essay.
He was gray, draped heavy, tee-shirt, buzz cut clean
and carved cheeks. He explained
his under-funded Veteran's hospital stay
trying to regain the use of his knee
and his voice — tired metal.
I explained commas and sentence
fragments — he listened patiently,
but something about his clenched chest
and the feeling I was speaking to him
through a 6 inch sheet of glass
shrank all the places where I tried to breathe
and I was sweating
like the Fallujah heat
was still radiating
from his pale cheeks.

I wanted something more to say to him
and it wasn't like me, not at all really,
I don't know how to speak to hands
imprinted with the weight of an M16 for my safety,
hands with grit of sand still sunken
in the cracks and surely I don't know
how to speak to eyes that were smothered
with desert on all sides so immense
it seemed there could be no end and that
it could swallow him.
Even if I didn't want him to, he fought for me.
And I don't even know how to speak to feet
that know the crunch of shrapnel, glass, and splinters
of market stand. I don't know much of anything
about what scratched into his veins or where it's buried
or what things he carried, if it was auburn hair fluttering in the breeze
or *Yea, though I walk through the valley...* that sustained him.

I don't know what to say to him
when a car door slammed too hard or a sudden thunder clap
jams his heart against his back.
All I know is... in another life,
my hands and my privilege are his
and his only way into college
would be my ticket into his thicker skin.
So I looked at this boy, my age or less,
and with stumbling lips
I thanked him.

I thanked him

and the cut of his eyes lodged in me.
Like *convince*. Like *justify*. But my tongue
has swan dived down my throat.
I just wanted him to not look so alone
sitting right across from me. So I thanked him
because I hadn't seen him smile yet
and I wanted to see that.
Because there are dark places where chest plates cave in
after too many explosions and I might never have to go there.
Because I am safe *daily*
and I might never know the fear of turning a corner to find a bullet
with my face on it.
Or I just wanted to make conversation.
Or I just wanted him to give me
any small reason to believe he was okay.
Maybe I should have said, *I'm sorry.*
Maybe I should have said nothing
but I thanked him.
His face twisted disbelief, mine too.
The world is not so simple
that I can save people with *thank you's.*
All I gave him was a handful of spent shell casings:
words he didn't want like
Thank you rocket missing by inches
thank you splinters (for what)
thank you ghosts of stones

thank you bumper stickers
thank you coming home (for what)
thank you glass bottle
thank you stop loss
thank you flag-draped box (for what)
thank you right across from me
thank you hands shaking
thank you heart jammed back
thank you conversation
thank you scratched veins
thank you sustain him
thank you cracks
thank you wrong place
thank you caved in
for what...

I thank him – and everything goes tunnel vision,
and he cranes his head a little to the left
and the silence tastes like smoke
and something between us is unraveling and he's 1000
yards and gazing
so I thank him
and he says

For what?

For what...

Blood Is, at Once, Your Ugliest and Most Honest of Mirrors: A Triptych

I.

On the 4th day God created America
said let there be white
and saw that it sprawled like bleach
to taste all corners   plant its acid kiss on each ocean
leave buffalo bones in the sun clean stripped
and bodies left swinging from trees then
and even the blankets were poison
the starter pistol barked while wrapped
in porcelain fingers   all bets were off
and all deals were broken
an acid kiss on each ocean
and heels spur spiked into the bellies of horses
and the natives marched until their feet opened
like a choir   they were crushed under
America born like a hospital dropped onto them
from the heavens   called them sick
savages but the sick were in charge
the sickness churned
America carved a red and blue wound in a southern dust chest
splayed and tinkered with   flags planted in it
a calves' heart in a butcher's shop window
the butcher stole the shop
the butcher wears a white smock
the butcher confuses people with livestock
the grain crop sways like a tired mother
whose husband and child were sold away
reach your hands into the open cavity somewhere in the country's
center
cup the wild beating bulb knot heart of conquer and chain and believe
in free in pain
and squeeze and know
                    this is where you came from
                    this is where you came

2.
Noise:
Cries from the belly
of a ship or the belly of the ocean. A bustle of promise
in Ellis Island, broken. Tony said something about millions
of truths. The screech of liquid steel poured. The punch
of a machine molding doors for Ford sedans or a machine's
crunching bite through the bone lattice on the back of a man's hand.
The slosh of Ben Roger's brush whitewashing
a barb toothed border fence.
A blue siren's twist. A preacher wrapping Leviticus
like a grenade in his fist.
Fingernails mad scratch on the glass beneath my feet.
The glass beneath my feet
cracking.
The hushed mumble of men moving in the reinforced glass
at night. The slide click in the middle of a mixing board.
Fingerpick blues and needle tick.
A metronome countdown to Armageddon or upswell –
the choir waves, undulates, sings. A continuous loop of a judge
reading the Rodney King verdict. The wet slap of a tongue
sleepwalking into the night.
The rustle of a hand slipping up the back of a puppet. The other
clicking back the hammer. The click of channel.
The click of casket lid.
The click of stripper's heels on a glass floor.
The clink of champagne glasses
in well manicured hands. Adderall rattling in bottles.
Cartoons making fun of the government. A kiss
limping in the wind, hungering. Knees, teeth, and knuckles grinding.
Attempted communion cheering 100,000 deep
in a football stadium. Clean water whispering to the bottom of a glass.
A history professor droning.
The students talking softly as they're leaving.
The burst of an atomic bomb opening over a calm city. A plane
slamming open
a new mouth
in a building.

3.
First I place you in the widest of fields
because this is where you have always been.

Then I place you knees down, palms up
asking forgiveness,
then I build.

IV.
HOME

Pep Talk
After Gahl Liberzon

Speak *wow*. She's mysterious. Disinterested.
Eyes speak a little damage.
Look at her eyes. She's looking back. Holy crap.
She's smiling. Speak why? No wait,
get your hands outta your pockets. No leave 'em in.
Forget your hands. Speak. Forget. Look
she moves like a dolphin on an underwater slip n' slide coated in butter
and what does that even mean?
Speak emerald eyes really pretty can't stop looking. Stop
looking, I mean staring, what you're doing is definitely staring but look,
dear sweet lord she's still smiling and her breasts
are really nice even under that sweatshirt, don't look at them
but God if you could just peel that off and... no, now's not the time.
Speak you're a poet, no, she'll look right through that.
Speak family, fragments and philosophy,
no, speak her.
Stop looking at your feet.
Words needed, signals the tongue. Brain pees itself and runs.
Speak the light caresses her like dew on lilies' lips and oh
can you imagine your lips all over her...no don't
imagine your tongue at the pearly gates of her teeth
go easy on the worship speak
her story looks beautiful but you could spend an eternity
reading the cover over and over.
Do you believe in love at first
speak your hunger to her
fumble for words
look in her eyes
breathe break dive sigh
speak
Hi...

Notes on Touching a Woman

I will run my tongue across your scars
like a gondola gliding through Venice,

hold you as rain dancing across Main Street
holds street lamps' glow like a freshly kissed cheek.

My hands blush before your body —
sky and anguish compressed to flesh turn
moment to wine turns inhibition to wind to song
that could mirage an oasis in
the desert throat of a man.

I am a child reading the hymnals
of your freckles. I will
swim
my fingers across your shoulders —
a school of minnows.

Your eyelids are hummingbird wings.
Your collarbones are the legs of Sandhill Cranes.
Your hips are church bells, so ring —
bring me to my knees, on this day,
on this ground, bring sound like
sounds like your twirl in a purple dress
shroud and flourish
of Tao
like all that ever was is
now
touching
you.

I will massage your sore back and calves
like you deserve,
kiss your stomach like your belly button is a fountain of youth,
trace your spine like the wind on the side of the Eiffel Tower.

When I touch you
I'm a lost explorer
and my nights survival of cold
depends upon striking the match of your pleasure
and the soft flicker of my matchstick in the wind
is the space between my fingers and your skin.

This is how I tremble:
when you are naked —
a cloudless sky
falling
blazing.

I will tuck my lips' fear behind the curve of your ear.
I will whisper my dreams into the valley behind your knee.

I will hold the rocks of your bruises between my teeth.
I will leak
sap from the knots in my arteries and knees.

Your breath is a plume of smoke from a flute.
Your moans are diaphanous sheets of sonata.
Your voice is red silk sliding across marble.

Your gaze
turns me on
and boils
my bones.

Here

After Aracelis Girmay

Here is the library of you, be quiet.
People are trying to forget things.
Here are your insecurities– a giant
inflatable purple gorilla tethered
to the roof of your used car lot of loneliness.

Because your 2nd place trophies
warm the benches of confidence,
the sting of every F swells on your report card,
and your fucked up people skills
sink through every party you attend
like a lump of shit in a bubble bath.

Here is the first time somebody called you ugly,
your shell in pieces at your feet,
and your naked ass of enlightenment.

This is your poetry —
a decapitated male praying mantis
humping the air in an act of blind faith.
These are your failings:
sticky notes pasted to the insides your eyelids.
Here is your head as a leaking fishbowl.
Here are the rocks of your apologies.
Here, your sister holds an empty coloring book
and your heart melts to crayon wax.
Here is your father's raincoat, full of holes,
as the accusing sky in your mouth pours down.
Here are your brother's fists full of tears
that you taught him to hide in there,
and your mother's hands like old bread
brittle, cracked.
Here you are sweeping up the crumbs.

Here is every woman you've ever loved killing herself over
and over again and the goldfinch in your throat
singing to them to please stop.
The champagne flutes in their wrists cracked
when they clasped hands in prayer too hard.
Look, the shard lodged in your palm
reminds no matter how beautiful you write them
or how you try to encircle with arms
they will still rush into the dark
farther than you can chase with candle and spark.

Here was one chance to get everything perfect.
A gambler's paycheck life — pissed it away.
An ice water in rotten teeth life — soaked you awake.
This was wishing you had more words for him:
Your grandfather on his hospital bed —
the limbs strapped, the machines,
the pain in your stomach like a swarm of bees.
Alive. The honey pooled in your throat,
and your spine.

This was your time.
Here.
An ice cube puddled on the carpet,
but out of the stains, the ether, the knuckles split,
the love you sipped,
here is your alchemist. Yes,
he does exist.

Here are your family dinners —
the few without arguments.
Here are you and Allen at 7, cardboard sword fighting.
And the lake, and the lake, and lakes where days rippled —
and pretending to be Mario and Luigi with fire flowers and frog suits
and such big joy from small boys.
Here is a stand-up routine delivered in a Darth Vader helmet,
a room full of family laughing so hard they're gasping
and crying and stomping,
and church is what you feel like.

Here are the AK's busting raps
and a storm that keeps you in
and a storm that you kept in for too long
that made you sing.
Here is your lover on the porch swing humming
to the autumn wind to warm it.
Here is everything you will never forget
and the many things you will.
Blessed.

For Dad

You come home bruised.
Exhaustion smokes through you
and I don't open the window of your mouth.
Struggling others empty their stories
into your head,
a bed of splinters.

Stress lines settle there
like Pittsburgh rivers.

I am daily business and a loudmouth television,
missing this chance
to listen.

I am looking for the right words or hands to fix
anything, but mine know best
the last kiss of baseball stitch leaving fingertips.
This is what you gave me
and what I have to give.

I wear the gifts of your name,
a body, and a brain sometimes
used to train a slingshot mouth
with stones with blame to thud against your
wide chest I was gladly buried in.

But you gave me this roof, the light by which I write,
the kind mornings, this warm bed,
the Red Wings parade, the widest day,
air fives, the last few minutes,
the coke spray hollering celebration,
these memories we wrestle in,
and the million small kindnesses that a child forgets.

Dad, this is the offertory part of the poem,
so pay attention. Here it is. Forgiveness.

We fucked up a bunch of times.   It happens. This is a *thank you*
to alight in your ear when you forget. A *thank you*
because you deserve to know you succeeded.
You packed my mouth with stories,
cried in front of me, and tied my skates.
Parents so rarely get to hear that they've done right.
And I maybe one day I'll understand the splinters
of your heart   that are mine
that I am so lucky to find
and begin to pull them from my palms
and watch them shine.

It Is a Memory of Thirsting

My mother says sound travels farther
over water. I like this, imagine
yelling across to the other side
as if I could see my own voice
rippling on the surface.

I'm just live water, clay softening, eggshells,
gunpowder erupting kiss bloom through skull,
ecstatic fabric, the taste of metal
from the well, the amniotic sky, a shower of skin and days.

In my family we always seem to find our way
to a lake. And listen there and wait
and pray.

The water wakes and asks what time it is.
The body wakes and asks for a glass to sip.
The boy wakes and asks for his father,
the feeling of granite. The church,
granite. The erosion happens. *The spin
and leap. Alive, we're alive.* Splash
your hands against me. Dissolve me
in your vast arm span.

The girl at poetry camp builds walls of sand
on the playground. Then washes them away.
She says, *Watch. No matter how big I build the wall
the water still washes it away.*

Thom says *in rainbows* beneath *blank shore*
and it's almost imperceptible.

I'm evaporating at the knees.

I like to wade. I like spaghetti.
I like to quote the Simpsons constantly.

I like the words dissipate and evanesce.
I like my family.
I like to cry when things are slipping from me.

My throat contracts in attempt
to crush water from the stone at its center.

What are we but a confluence
of rivers, stories, and electricity?
We are pornography and pressing bodies,
for they are memories of longing.

And I've seen people kiss,
a brilliant mist. My eyelids
are water-logged ceilings caving in.
I drip away slowly, like promises
tumbling into a strange puddle
I once saw my face reflected in.

I Know I Can't Have You

but I pray one day our atoms
are recycled in a way
that allows us to touch

or some physics of multiple universes
gives me one chance
to rub the knots of the day
from the creases of your shoulder blades.

That's not enough.

I know I can't have you
so let me have a single evening,
watching cartoons watching
your comfort as it blooms.

Let me catch my breath
stalling in my throat
like a scared child in a classroom
hiding behind coats.

Let me go back to the moment
so long since
you rushed up and hugged me with so much energy
and said you missed me and I got nervous
and said some dumb shit. Instead,

let me say
the million lovely I missed you too's that
somersaulted through my body
like forsythia petals.
Let me say the right things.

I know I can't have you
so much, but if I could hold you
like a giant ragged sweatshirt

draped across your shoulders...

If I could only write this again
with the courage
to put your name in it
I could stop whispering your initials,
to my pillow.

Maybe, I could stop folding your smile
into my irises' origami
in hopes that it might open
in my dreams.

Let me imagine a world
where I can hold your hand
and watch the ceiling fan.

Your presence brings moth wings to my neck.
Sometimes this is enough to let me rest.

Your eyes are the secrets
raindrops tell the clouds
before they fall.

In Relation to Her Hands

I'm losing my grip as tickling drifts to distance.
She's in Disney Channel plastic dreams I can't stand to see.
Still, she's balance beaming at me
and I'm not sure how to tell her
she still glows like little sister.
I come home with teeth like excuses,
telling myself I can't bridge the space between us,
cannot make bead designs to melt in the oven,
listen to her bow sweep over viola strings,
or lift her to shake the ceiling fan with laughter.
What do you do when they go teenage?
Brothers are easy.
You watch some cartoons and wrestling,
swear at each other and teach him to shave.
But she's complicated. We're untied shoelaces,
I'm fumbling like I've never seen fingers before.
In relation to my sister, I'm a ghost protector
trying to grow flesh and backbone,
and offer to paint her nails,
or paint something beautiful with her
get on my knees and paint like
this is you, this is me
there's my selfishness shed in the corner.
Here are your dimples rising in sparrows' wings.
Here's I'm proud of you, and always will be
brushed across my eyes
like light.

The Last Song

The day broke into
showers of light staining upturned faces.

Trees bent their arms to massage the earth.
Tires screeched attempted harmonies.

The wind whispered deafening
over traffic and drunken mumbles.

Smog chased its tail - so cute
I wanted to eat it up.

I folded my failures into paper airplanes,
sailing out of sight.

The weight of the world
went sledding down my back.

My cadence crumbled away — a canyon's edge.
My bones were scarecrow sticks.

My dust storm of cells fell into the shallow end of youth
and resurfaced with arm-fulls of time.

My smile was a ship in a bottle. My smile
was stapled to my face like a flier for a long forgotten concert.

My smile was a secret admirer chasing you
with a bouquet of kisses.

Clouds consumed city lights veiling
the moon, solemn on the doorstep,

afraid to knock
the world off kilter.

The street lamps dripped fireflies.
The northern lights ate the sky.

Polaris walked me to the door
but refused

to spend the night
in my arms.

snapshot physics and the end of the universe

when a warm wind brushes a girl holding a dandelion
and ruffles her dress
and rafts tufts of seedlings into a sky
the moment aches and immediately
freezes into a snapshot behind
what might be god's eyes
the universe breaks a heavy sigh
and the silent furnaces
where atoms grow up
turn like dust

there are many things that exist
rather than nothing
she sweeps into them
on days like this

and today they say the end of existence will be cold
it will shiver slowly from the inside out
no spectral blue shift   no stars crashing to kingdom
come   no big crunch
we never get to collapse into
one   I don't want to let go of this
they say space is speeding up and leaving us

and she begins to hum

at the end
the center of endlessness
will burst like a rampaged heart   and each night
less and less stars in the sky

we will be less than bones
gravity will be an echo
and the earth will splinter away
in a gown of frost

but today there is a girl
and a sun   in waves   a wind that sways
and what will become of her hands
scraped raw on the day
her shoelace got caught in her bike chain
watching her mother put on make-up
the cold scissor tinged neck   her first haircut
her red journal with gold latch
her mouthful of things to say
the first raindrop on her wrist
from the storm that once made her afraid
watching her friend Lily shrink from view
with her cheek on the car window
her aspiration to eventually
get really good at bowling
and how she always ran in the dark
when no one was around

where then go her stories and the air that carried them?
how might these have slipped to emptiness?

if she sings and no one's around
does it still ache in my marrow?

I can't let go of this
when some day infinite
when a girl's dress is ruffled by the wind
and there is drifting
and god might be filing the moment away for safe-keeping
and the stars are patting each other on the back
and smoking cigars
everything might be in its right place
and that is lightning striking repeatedly
beneath my teeth
and I walk on water
but it's inside my body
and I am going home
and she is there holding hands with my mother
and one day it will all crumble

and be smoke or ash or ice or nothing
and these words will be the dead skin cells
of the moon

I only hope that on that day I will be allowed
to reach behind what might be god's eyes
hold that snapshot in my hands and say
yes   there was beauty
I was there   it blazed through me
even now in dark glass gelatin and the clock melt of memory
impressed somewhere   a photograph of everything
I can't stop from disappearing
but I might hold that thin film of chemical and see
a daydream of my mother and the girl
maybe a garden   maybe a breeze
and she might hold an inchworm on her fingertip
and she might climb a tree
and she might shake the branches
watch the clouds sleep   wake the leaves
and I will dream
and I will dream
of all
that might be

Regression Therapy

I think of the billions of people wandering
across the earth – who I will never know.
Multiply them by the cavernous vault
of space. The sickening immensity.
The runaway madness of pinpricked stars
and their distant brothers whose
light ferments empty.
This cold, logic, vacuum, telescopes,
unbearable vastness.

I imagine all of it
concentrated to a single point of infinite density
in my mother's eyes.
And I try to remember what it's like to be new

and smile.

Carry Me In

After Pablo Neruda

Open those mouths of oceans. Ingest
my soft cells, my body. I want to know
the loose crumbles of dirt
in my cradled skull.

When my slung satchel
of heart empties its pages
and goes silent, carry me
home.
Skywash the ink from my hands. Do not
curl into fists,
my bones.

I know with no self
there is no alone.
So let me have sleepovers with rain.

I know the wind
will forget my name
but let me play tag with the leaves for the rest of the day.

Carry me in
like an eroding
shoreline.

I just want to un-clench
like a fallen branch.

There is so much to hold
in these knots of shoulders,
in this tome of tongue
where all memories curl under,
in these wheels of knees
spokes snap

hold me.

Carry me in like the end of a long dream.

Let my ribs hug the earth.
Let my love soak into this world
like light from dingy flickering bulb
hanging on a thin string

I want to sink away like the night in a clay pot
in the yard. Grow something green and verdant
in the place where my flesh went.
So many apologies,
I am winded.

Carry me to the places where my words sleep
and let me join them.

The footsteps sadly drum.
Carry my eyes away
cell by cell
until they stare blindly in every direction
at the same time
and see nothing at all.
Let something drink
from the chalice of my sunken stomach.

Air hold me fast.
Earth carry me in.
In your mouth
and in your hands.

Windspeak me empty.

Those who loved me know
I fell apart good
and gently.

V.
THE
ODD
MC

The Ill Lad and The Odd MC

we called it rockin' the cock and balls:

to record our raps
we had
a microphone wedged between
two small round computer speakers
which looked suspiciously like...well...
I'd like to think
we were pioneers
in the field of audio engineering

a jury rig of mic and tape deck
from a karaoke machine
found in Erik's parent's basement
was enough to capture vocals laced with
gravel from the mouths of shy kids
titans standing on 808 kicks
it was something so sacred
to hear and hold our creation
with beats stolen from the internet
papers in our fists
slashes where the bars end/
artistry snuck in like this/
from the sound when gats bust to the churn
of stomach from a step dad's punch
from ultra-violence and disassembled bodies
to acupuncture of what made us ugly
from songs about the size of our nuts
to how does it feel
to scrawl alien art on the walls of a faceless city
to be small
to be nobody
to play the piano softly   off key

we turned the rusted the tumblers in our throats
found stories in the fragments lodged in our teeth

pulled imagination from the cobwebs
brought voice to throw
at the walls of a faceless city
to colorize a whitewashed suburban no-place
to do something with your best friend
besides watch TV and play video games
and cure the cancer of middle class malaise
the empty schools the drain
the carpet of childhood that can never be un-stained

we lived to have a craft
to find the word
to resuscitate the tongue
to still write rhymes to this day like
yes yes ya'll -- I still rock the cock and balls
like I rock my awkward flaws/
and E will spit 1 verse
that'll make your grandma take off her bra/
and the stage is what she'll toss it on/
sorry, I almost lost it ya'll

to find a voice in a junkyard of rims and gold teeth
to polish it   to spit
to hear the beat drop and think
yes
for the weird kids to get Ill
for the Ill kids to get sick
the best days of my life were spent
in a bland white room
with my best friend
with 2 pads and 2 pens
throwing our guts soft red
our failings   desires
and the scrap metal of our heads
against a beat
until we ran out of breath

and said
play that shit again.

MICHAEL "BOOKS" MORIARTY, a.k.a. Verbal Assault, Cuddles Afterwords, and The Southern Dandy—was born and resides in Ann Arbor, Michigan, where he is a member of the spoken word poetry group Wordworks. He is the 2008 Ann Arbor Slam Champion, the recipient of two Gold Crown Awards in free-form poetry from Columbia University, and has taught and performed in schools across the state of Michigan. KRISTIN STELTER PHOTO

Acknowledgements

MY THANKS TO the editors of publications in which these poems first appeared:

Blood Orange: "Regression Therapy," "It Is a Memory of Thirsting"
The Huron River Review: "The Last Song," "Notes on Touching a Woman," "Wading," "In Relation to Her Hands"

THESE THANK YOU'S are going to take a long time, so you may want to get some snacks.

I would like to thank Ann Arbor Wordworks, and all of its founding members. I'd also like to thank the WW poets who I've had the joy of working with: Angel Nafis, Daniel Bigham, Maggie Ambrosino, Gahl Liberzon, Claire Forster, Langston Kerman, Courtney Whittier, Peggy Boroughs, Matt Dagher-Margosian, Toniesha Jones.

I am grateful to the 2007 Ann Arbor National Slam team, as well as the entire A2 slam, for their wisdom, support, and hard work: Karyna McGlynn (from the top, not from the...), Logic (Tiny Dancer), Matt Ernst (Curtis Longstroke), Deb Marsh, Larry Francis, and Erik Daniel, I am in awe of your art, and in debt of your kindness. And thanks for my very first poet nickname. Thanks to the 2008 Ann Arbor Youth Slam Team: Ben Alfaro, Tony Zick, Fiona Chamness, Aimee Lee, Carolyn Blessing, and Marshall Thomas. I hope you learned half as much from me as I did from you. You put up with my hater ways.

Thank you to the Neutral Zone and all of its staff and supporters.

My appreciation to the Washtenaw Community College Poetry Club, and all of my friends from the Writing Center: Joey Sims, Malcolm Barrett, Zach Baker, Maggie Hanks, Matt Hunter, Anthea Schroeder, Bushra Malaibari, Joe Klein, Joe Montgomery, Mary Mullaly, Deborah Bayer.

To all my excellent teachers and mentors: Tracy Komarmy, Michelle Mountain, Ron Miller, Charles Avinger, Max Gibson, Esther Hurwitz, thank you for your courage, guidance, and skill.

Immense gratitude to the poets who've done so much for me and my craft: Roger Bonair-Agard, Patrick Rosal, Ross Gay, Kevin Coval (for your insightful editing on the beginning of this book), Scott Beal, and Aracelis Girmay – never did I dream I'd work with such inspired and brilliant people.

Thanks to my friends, the poetry community, and those who have supported me: Brian Wakeman, Phil Cochran, Jamie Killen, Ben Detlefs, Hannah Curtis, Hilary Wolkan, Stephanie Custer, Lauren Weston, Malika Middlebrooks, Haley Cureton, Kat Bayless, Jimmy Bock and Donna Angelo, Kent Klausner, Lizzy Gitterman, Deondre Richmond, Taylor Smith, Sarah Kow-Falcone, Paul Vites, Tom Syzmanski,

Josh Wise, Arhm Choi, Maria Gresiak, Alden Taint, and Cooper Mulholland, The Sweetwater's Writers Reading, especially Don Hewlett and Chris Lord for your unwavering support.

Scott and Steve Stelter, I am grateful for your acceptance and kindness.

I'd like to recognize the inprising artists noted in this book, as well as Radiohead, The Simpsons, King of the Hill, South Park, and Futurama. Aesop Rock, Sole, Blackalicious, El-P, Dose One, Deep Puddle Dynamics, Juvenile, The Cash Money Millionaires, The X-Files, Gillian Anderson, Bob Dylan, Leonard Cohen, Cee-lo Green, Goodie Mob, Subterraneous Records, Sage Francis, Krs-One, Jeff Mcdaniel, Saul Williams, and Wesley Willis.

Saroyan Humphrey, thank you for your vision, and help in making this a reality.

Enormous thanks to Erik Rogers (aka the supervillian) for the AK's, Arcane, the friendship and inspiration, and the fact that were it not for our mad rhymes, I wouldn't be writing this.

Thank you Tom Zimmerman for your unending generosity, for your work on this book, all your contributions to poetry and to me, and for being a great friend and mentor.

Jeff Kass, thank you for seeing potential in me, for your incredible teaching, for editing this, and for the ubiquitous impact your passion and work have had on me and this community.

Jas Obrecht, thank you so much for your faith in me. Your friendship means worlds. Your are a singular and symphonic human being. I am humbled to share in this craft with you. May all good things find their way into your wisest of hands. R.I.P. Psycho.

To the Rutkowskis, Bocks, Fesslers, and Moriartys, I hope I can return your love and support. Chris and Kathleen, I am proud to be your brother. I am guided by your luminous futures. Paul Bock, (Ralphies! RELOAD!) Mom and Dad, thank you, thank you, thank you, and on and on. I am awed by your sacrifices and love. You've done so much for me it can't possibly be written here. Thank you for compassion. For teaching me how to cry and laugh, and sometimes both.

Kristin, I would crumble without you. Thanks for helping me believe when the wild hounds of doubt were chewing on my tatters. You are so beautiful, talented, so compassionate, and tolerant of my antics. Let's raise a cup of sunrise and moonshine to our lips and taste what used to be distance. I love you.